How To Manage Your Money

A Comprehensive Reference For Financial Novices On Budgeting, Money Management, Prudent Expenditure, Debt Management, And Long-Term Investment Strategies

(How To Boost Your Income Online Without Investing Or Developing Any Skills)

BayramWindisch

Getting Ready for Change

"We cannot progress if we are unable to adjust. Without growth, we cease to exist."

Reaching for a better financial situation also presents plenty of opportunities for resistance because it drives ongoing internal and external changes. Most people who aspire to riches resist change even though they desire their lives to improve because they find comfort in their relatively predictable financial patterns. Conditioning exercises are a part of many workout programmes because they help the body adapt to new muscular motions and cognitive demands. Similarly, an effective programme for preparing for financial fitness includes actions that lessen the discomforts associated with financial situations.

However, they achieve financial freedom and contentment because they are unwilling to tolerate temporary discomfort. Fortunately, by understanding the reasons behind your resistance and making a proactive plan for change, you can gradually alter the deeply rooted beliefs, attitudes, feelings, and actions that keep you in your current financial circumstances.

Dangers Shown by the Identity Factor

She was paying off her debt and developing sound financial practices, but one of the reasons for resistance is what you called the Identity Factor. This defence mechanism protects a person's sense of self and place in the universe. People usually avoid making the necessary adjustments when this happens or fall back on old habits, protecting their comfortable lifestyle at all costs for fear that when the changes eventually come about, they would make them feel uncomfortable, frightened, and con

formulated a plan with the assistance of a credit counsellor to pay off her debt, stop using credit cards, and keep better financial records.

She was so excited about the progress she saw after three months of strict adherence to the programme that she stopped keeping a budget out of embarrassment, but in the fourth month, she began to fall behind on her payments and had to borrow money from friends twice. Six months later, she was back where she had been six months earlier, with additional debt, a propensity to put off handling money matters, and a confused understanding of her spending.

When Celine first called me, she was angry with herself for standing in the way of her progress.

She discovered that her acts were self-protective rather than self-sabotaging once she realised that she had been safeguarding her previous identity by turning to behaviours that had more predictable results.

She gradually started to grow and learn how to deal with the discomfort brought on by her altered behaviours, both of which enabled her to stick to her budget.

Significant change can damage someone's sense of self, and it can also have an impact on relationships with peers and family of origin.

People recognise you for who you used to be, so any changes you make to your attitudes or behaviours force them to react to you differently, which causes them to change as well.

Unchangeable friends or family members could try to stand in your way of success, making you feel even more miserable because you will believe you are the only one.

Fortunately, you'll learn that being alone is not inevitable as you prepare for change.

You can revisit past acquaintances and friendships and create new connections with people who reflect your changing identity and who will unavoidably come into your life.

Acknowledging the Moving Dumbers: If you have ever moved, you have undoubtedly encountered the "moving stupids." It can be perplexing to begin transitioning to new financial circumstances and behaviours because the outcome and the path are both uncertain.

Ailment

The symptoms include feeling overloaded, confused, lost, and alone, as well as a tendency to misplace items or make poor decisions.

However, the discomforts of moving into a new home gradually subside as your spending habits improve, and you become used to your new surroundings.

By acknowledging the moving stupids as a step towards a better financial situation, you can decrease their duration and move forward. When he reached fifty, he got ready to reassess his relationship with money.

He felt indebted and was embarrassed about his lack of financial literacy despite his desire for financial stability. Agreed to follow a spending plan we developed, stop using his credit cards when he started working with me, and keep track of every dollar he spent.

He whined, "I've got a terrible case of the moving stupids." I'm afraid I'll make a mistake in my calculations and spend too much.

Also, when I jot down my daily expenses, it feels like another person inhabits my body. This isn't how I normally behave. Told me after a further two weeks that his new behaviours were more natural and that the perplexity and anxiety were gradually going away.

However, he had fleeting epiphanies whenever he implemented a new habit, like setting aside money each pay period.

But he knew the moving stupids were a sign of maturity and would soon stop, so he was ready to go through the experience.

Activities

The following actions can help you become more self-aware, which will help you overcome resistance and prepare for change. You practise patience and make progress. To double your efforts, acclimatise to little changes before tackling larger ones.

1. Start a Prosperity Diary.

Use it to convey your sentiments about change, write down your fears or reluctance, acknowledge your victories, and underline any questions. This will allow you to define your current state and track your development as you strengthen your financial muscles.

Dating each item facilitates a more comfortable analysis of your findings in the future.

2. Locate a Prosperity Partner

Collaborating with a friend might boost your drive to lessen pain and create a more enjoyable transfer to a new financial situation.

Designate a person you feel comfortable discussing personal matters regularly for your experience-sharing sessions—for example, once or twice a week.

During each one, take turns talking about any discomforts you've experienced (such as estrangement or disorientation), noting your progress from the previous session, soliciting criticism if you'd like, and outlining what you'll do before the next one. It's best to avoid criticising your friend's behaviour or giving uninvited advice, as this could lead to conflict.

Rather, encourage your friend by emphasising their successes. Selecting prosperous friends outside of your relationship is a great choice for couples, particularly if you often have emotional conversations about money. You can work through financial issues with your partner, but confiding in a third party will probably encourage you to be more forthright and honest about issues. People who use the buddy system progress faster than those who don't.

Talking about financial behaviour is an uncommon method that helps people express themselves more honestly and often significantly reduces the discomfort associated with financial behaviour. 3. Determine who you are financially.

Your financial identity is shaped by your attitudes, convictions, emotions, behaviours, and financial relationships.

You may identify early warning indicators of resistance to financial change and handle the uncertainty that will inevitably surface as your financial status improves by clearly grasping your financial identity. List all the components of your financial identity as you perceive them in your prosperity diary, allowing room for adjustments in the future.

5. Always practise using reserve funds.

It doesn't seem to be very enjoyable to put money aside. But if you master the subject, you'll be more equipped to handle both the good and the bad moments of daily life. Moreover, you'll get better the more you save.

With repetition and time, tendencies take on a structure. Every dollar you save contributes to this new way of thinking and doing. It could be easier to save the next $1.

Never forget that you are attempting something truly novel. But acknowledge that you are forming a habit that will follow you for the rest of your life.

The Mental Factors Influencing Spending Behaviours

A young woman named Emily used to reside in the thriving Metropolis of Metropolis. Emily was a bright, dynamic person who had just received her college degree and landed a lucrative job. She was thrilled to have achieved financial independence and was eager to sample the results of her hard work.

But when handling her finances, Emily had a flaw: she was prone to making rash purchases.

She could not resist the temptation to indulge whenever she passed the plentiful windows of upscale fashion retailers or the inviting scent of freshly brewed coffee from snug cafes.

Emily's emotional spending patterns were mostly motivated by her need for approval and rapid satisfaction. Emily had always felt alienated as a child. She often makes comparisons between herself and her wealthier friends, who appear to be able to afford opulent trips and stay up-to-date with fashion.

Whenever Emily bought something, she experienced a little surge in her self-esteem and a momentary sense of fulfilment. Her fears were briefly overshadowed by the thrill of obtaining something new, which gave her the appearance of acceptance and belonging in society. Emily sought affirmation from other people's praise and confused material belongings with personal worth.

Emily found breaking the pattern of this emotional attachment to spending challenging. It was a means of satisfying the emptiness and escaping the underlying sentiments of inadequacy. She persuaded herself that dining at hip restaurants or possessing the newest designer purse would make her happier and more content.

Over time, Emily's reckless spending began to negatively impact her capacity to manage her finances. She was having trouble making ends meet and was running up credit card debt. Although she understood in her heart that her spending was unsustainable, she found it difficult to resist the emotional appeal of rapid pleasure.

Emily once had a recommendation to read a piece about the psychology of spending patterns and the feelings that motivate them. For her, it served as a wake-up call. She saw that her excessive spending was not providing her with the contentment and happiness she desperately wanted. Rather, it generated a vicious cycle of fleeting euphoria, financial strain, and guilt.

To alter her connection with money, Emily embarked on a path of introspection and development. She started investigating her underlying emotional demands and looked for more healthful means of meeting them. She began to cultivate an appreciation for the wealth in her life by engaging in mindfulness and gratitude practices.

In addition, Emily sought assistance from those who shared her financial security goals. She became involved in internet forums devoted to personal finance and acquired knowledge about investing, saving, and budgeting. She gained financial control and a sense of empowerment over time.

Emily began implementing mechanisms to stop her impulsive spending as she became more aware of her emotional drives. She meticulously tracked her spending and allocated funds to her top priorities as she established her budget. She developed the ability to distinguish between needs and wants and made deliberate choices about using her money.

Emily eventually realised that connections and experiences, not things, truly fulfilled her. She learned that lasting relationships and life-enriching events were the genuine sources of happiness rather than fleeting moments of possession.

Emily's spending patterns changed over time from being impulsive to deliberate. She learned to be more aware of her emotional triggers and knew when to stop shopping as an emotional crutch or to look for approval from others. Rather, she concentrated on creating a life that reflected her ideals and discovering happiness in the little things.

As the years went by, Emily became financially secure and developed a strong sense of fulfilment and self-worth. She realised that her spending habits were now motivated by her internal ideals and objectives rather than by approval from others. Emily inspired others by sharing her experience and guiding others through navigating their emotional motives behind spending habits.

Is there someone Emily reminds us of? Most likely You!

Ultimately, Emily's narrative serves as a reminder that long-term financial well-being depends on comprehending our emotional impulses and cultivating a positive connection with money. True fulfilment in life can only be attained by breaking free from the cycle of impulsive spending via self-awareness, introspection, and deliberate choices.

How to improve your ability to manage finances

If you want to become more proficient at handling finances, take a look at these:

1. Learn accounting.

Finances by learning effective techniques for budget distribution, predictions, and readiness through an instructional budgeting course. These courses might include materials that let you practise creating budgets and assessing their efficacy. Online budgeting courses, as well as workshops and lectures, are available.

2. Acquire proficiency with accounting software

Although spreadsheets remain a popular tool for budget management, administrators can now improve their budget management abilities with the help of new technology. Certain budgeting software can produce expense reports, assess information, forecast revenue, and carry out mathematical operations to ensure accurate financial data.

3. Examine consistent financial success

Regularly assessing your budget's efficacy will help you become a better budget manager. Monthly assessments might assist you in creating fresh plans for handling money and making money. Performance can be assessed using prior budget records and quantified by consulting the financial data.

Advice for applying your skills in financial management at work

To assist you in effectively applying your financial management abilities at work, consider the following suggestions:

Discover several budgeting techniques: There are other ways to set aside money for spending, such as activity, zero-based, and progressive budgets. Acquiring many skills might provide you with a more effective toolkit to handle various situations at work.

Establish a system for documentation: A thorough approach to documentation, such as tracking expenses and providing invoices, can help establish your team's budgetary needs more easily.

Consult prior budgets: If you're unsure where to start with a budget or how to set up your budget management systems, look at prior budgets for ideas. Modifications can be made to fit your administrative style or current needs.

Receive your job alerts on Indeed.

Observe fresh opportunities in your area first.

How to highlight your ability to manage finances

Here are some ways to highlight these skills in an interview, a cover letter, and your resume:

Putting skills in financial management on a CV or cover letter

Cover letters and resumes are places to showcase your money management skills. When applying for a financial management job, understand the requirements by reading the job description. Using this information may make your cover letter and resume more unique while showcasing your skills. You can provide your prior job duties and a summary of your accounting experiences to further explain how you acquired your skills.

In an interview, talk about your ability to handle finances.

During an interview, you can highlight your proficiency in financial management by answering detailed questions. Interviewers frequently request detailed answers detailing instances in which you executed a skill related to budget management or effectively managed a budget. For the interviewer to assess your skills in action, they might also provide you with a fictitious budget report to review and analyse. An interview is another chance for you to highlight your communication abilities.

Developing a Powerful Brand

Crafting a Distinguished Brand Story: Embroidering Culinary Tales

Think of the brand for your food truck as an enticing story that draws customers in. Crafting an enduring brand narrative is akin to crafting a story that entices readers to explore your culinary universe. Your brand should communicate the tale of your journey, your love of flavours, and the distinctive experiences you provide, just like a chef infuses a story into each dish. Every aspect of your brand, from the story of your culinary explorations to the inspiration behind your trademark dish, should speak to your audience authentically and emotionally.

Creating a Professional Logo and Graphics: Identifying Visual Elements

Your food truck's logo and graphics are its public face in a world of visual impressions.

Creating a beautiful, delectable meal is similar to designing a good brand and visuals. The visual representation of your complete culinary concept, your logo is the soul of your business. The designs and colours you choose influence how people see your truck. Create your logo and graphics with meticulous attention to detail and a dedication to communicating the spirit of your business, just as a chef delivers a dish with care and delicacy.

Building an Internet Presence: Your Company's Digital Aromas

Think of the internet presence of your food truck as a scent that wafts through the internet, luring customers in. Creating an online presence is similar to using the digital realm to enhance your food offerings. Start by creating a website for your business, which can serve as a virtual storefront where clients can browse your menu, discover your history, and locate you. Next, embrace social media, which is word-of-mouth on the internet. Post mouthwatering pictures of your food, interact with viewers, and highlight the colourful character of your truck.

Online Ordering and Delivery Choices: Putting Convenience at the Fingertips of Customers

Convenience is a highly valued ingredient in today's cuisine. It's like bringing the table to the homes and offices of clients with online ordering and delivery choices. You can provide takeaway and delivery services through your website or other third-party channels, just like a chef would. It's about delivering your flavours to clients' doorsteps so they may enjoy your products more easily. Consider it as giving them a sneak peek into the wonder of your truck even when they cannot come in person.

Engagement with Customers and Loyalty Programmes: Building Strong Culinary Bonds

Think of the patrons of your food truck as valued guests and your efforts to engage them as the conversations that bring them back. One encounter at a time, relationship development is what customer engagement and loyalty programmes are all about. Interact with your followers on social media by leaving comments, soliciting their thoughts, and offering behind-the-scenes looks at your cooking adventures. Put in place loyalty programmes that give discounts to returning consumers; it's similar to a chef giving a regular client a free appetiser or dessert. These initiatives foster a feeling of gratitude and connection that keeps clients devoted and ready to return.

You may establish an emotional connection with your customers by crafting a compelling brand story. You can establish a visual brand that is just as delicious as your food using expert logos and graphic design. You're reaching a larger audience of possible clients when you have a solid web presence. You're accommodating modern convenience with online ordering and delivery choices. You're also cultivating relationships beyond sales by encouraging customer involvement and loyalty programmes. You're creating a digital ambience that elevates the experience of savouring your flavours, much like a chef elevates the dining experience. Your food truck offers more than just food as it enters the digital sphere; it's serving a multisensory experience that leaves an impression long after the last bite.

Practical Methods for Starting Self-Improvement in Chapter Three Work

Top Techniques for Enhancing and Developing Yourself

1. Regularly read

Books are specialised sources of information. The more books you read, the more wisdom you expose yourself to.

Daily book reading will increase the amount of knowledge in your brain.

2. Take a Language Course

As a Singaporean Chinese (a Chinese dialect), my three main languages are English, Mandarin, and Hokkien. I've recently started taking language classes—including Bahasa Indonesia and Japanese- out of curiosity.

I realised that learning a new language and culture is one of the best ways to better oneself and that mastering a language is a distinct skill.

3. Start a Novel Interest

Besides the things you usually enjoy doing, is there anything new you can learn? Is there something new you could take up?

You might also turn your new interest into a recreational activity. Dancing, Italian cuisine, Italian cooking, and ceramics.

Learning something new requires you to challenge yourself in many ways—mentally, physically, or emotionally.

(4) Sign up for a fresh course.

Attending courses is a great way to acquire new information and abilities. Short-term seminars, workshops, and online courses can all be beneficial in place of lengthy courses.

5. Create an Inspirational Environment

Your environment influences your emotions and behaviour. If you live in an inspiring atmosphere, you will be motivated every day.

A new coat of paint, some beautiful wall art, or some cosy furniture may make a room in your house seem less congested and more inviting. This will create an environment that will seem inspiring and warm all year round.

6. Overcome Your Fears

Your fears hold you back and impede you from changing for the better, whether it's a fear of risk, public speaking, or uncertainty.

Acknowledge that your concerns are a compass that indicates where you need to pay attention and where you may make progress.

7. Develop Your Capabilities

If you've ever played video games, you're probably aware of levelling up or acquiring skills to improve and get stronger.

8. Get up early

It's widely acknowledged that rising early improves quality of life and productivity.

If you get up early, you'll have time to improve yourself before others wake up. You'll extend your day, savour the quiet of the morning, and absorb sunlight, which will help your brain function.

9. Adhere to a Weekly Activity Plan

Being physically active can help you become more fit, making you a better person. I make it a point to jog three times a week, for at least thirty minutes each time.

10. Get Your Life Manual Started

A "life handbook" is a book that has all the information you need to live life to the fullest, including your purpose, beliefs, and goals. You may think of it as a manual on how to continuously improve so that you can lead the best possible life.

11. Write a letter to yourself later on.

Where do you envision yourself in five years? What kind of person will you become once you understand how to improve yourself?

Write a letter to yourself that you can later seal. Mark a date on your calendar to revisit it in a year or five. Then, when you open that letter, start becoming the person you want to be.

12. Step outside of your comfort zone.

True growth necessitates a great deal of sweat and work. Overindulgence in comfort stunts our growth and keeps us stagnant.

Establish the limits of your comfort zone and plan a systematic approach to gradually stepping outside it. Try cooking a dish you've never tried, hiking a trail you've never travelled on, or accepting a friend's invitation to go out when you normally say no.

13. Issue a challenge to an individual.

Competition is one of the best ways to grow and better oneself. Determine what your objective is (weight reduction, fitness, stable finances, etc.) and challenge a buddy who is passionate about the same things you are to see who can reach it first.

14. Identify Your Blind Areas.

According to research, blind spots are areas that are invisible to human sight. Regarding personal growth, blind spots are facets of ourselves that we are unaware of. Recognising our blind spots helps us to pinpoint the areas that still need improvement.

15. Seek out comments.

Regardless of our best efforts to improve, we will always have blind spots. Asking for feedback could help you see things differently and improve yourself.

Reaching out to friends, family, coworkers, supervisors, or even acquaintances is a wonderful idea because they can provide objective feedback without bias.

16. To help you focus, make to-do lists.

You can maintain focus by listing the tasks you wish to complete each day. Conversely, the days you don't accomplish this could be chaotic or ineffectual. You face the danger of forgetting certain things or running out of time because you haven't prepared how you will manage each one.

17. Set high standards for yourself

I support the use of BHAGs. Because they're bold and big, BHAGs force you to step outside your comfort zone in ways you wouldn't normally contemplate.

Which BHAGs can you undertake to feel proud of yourself once you've completed them? After setting them, start working on them.

18. Admit your mistakes

Everyone has flaws, but the most important thing is to recognise them, come to terms with them, and use self-improvement strategies to address them.

What do you think your shortcomings are? Which defects can you address immediately? How do you want to get in touch with them?

Remember to tackle this with self-love in mind. As you reflect on your shortcomings, try not to be cruel or rude to yourself. This is about pinpointing areas where you can improve, not what's wrong with you.

19. Show Courage

The most effective way to learn and improve is to act. What have you been wanting to get done for a while? How can you take prompt action?

20. Examine the Lives of the People Who Motivate You

Think about the people who inspire and awe you. These people are models of the qualities you want to have as you work on improving yourself.

Which qualities about them do you find admirable and wish you had yourself? How do these qualities come about?

21. Give Up a Bad Habit

Are there any bad habits you could try to get rid of? This can involve oversleeping, abusing alcohol or tobacco, or delaying chores.

22. Form a Novel Behaviour

Some great habits include reading books, rising early, exercising, reading a new personal development article daily, and practising meditation.

Things not to do

Certain behaviours or practices regarding time management can reduce your effectiveness and productivity. When it comes to time management, you should steer clear of the following:

Procrastination: Waiting until the last minute to do crucial activities can cause stress, hurried effort, and subpar results. To keep up productivity, don't put off work and take it on as soon as possible.

Overcommitting: Taking on excessive work or projects can cause inefficiency and overwhelm. When it comes to how much you can get done in a certain amount of time, be realistic and be able to say no.

Lack of prioritisation: Not setting priorities for your work can cause you to spend time on unimportant tasks and ignore vital ones. To ensure you're concentrating on the things that matter, rank your assignments according to their urgency and priority.

Inadequate planning: A vague daily plan or timetable might cause confusion and time loss. Spend time organising your work and schedule ahead of time, leaving some wiggle room in case something unforeseen arises.

Multitasking: Although it can make you appear productive, multitasking reduces your focus and efficiency. Trying to multitask frequently results in work that is of lower quality. Instead, give each task your whole attention and concentrate on it individually.

Ignoring self-care and breaks: Working nonstop without breaks can eventually cause burnout and a decline in productivity. Ensure your plan includes regular pauses to give yourself time to recover and focus.

Delegation is key. Attempting to handle everything by yourself might cause unneeded stress and overload. When acceptable, assign work to others and use your team's or colleagues' abilities and knowledge.

Ignorance of distractions: Distractions can seriously impair your productivity. Examples include social media, email notifications, and loud noises. Reduce distractions by utilising productivity apps, setting up a specific workstation, or shutting off notifications.

Inaccurate time estimate: Underestimating how long a task will take to finish can result in hurried effort or missed deadlines. When projecting how long each activity will take, be realistic and account for delays or unanticipated events.

Lack of adaptability: While having a plan and a timetable is necessary, being overly inflexible might make it difficult to adjust to changing conditions. Your timetable should be flexible to allow for unforeseen circumstances or changing priorities.

By staying away from these typical traps, you may become more proficient at managing your time, increase your output, and become more productive overall.

Practical Techniques for Personal Development: Self-esteem as a high school student. Adolescent life can be challenging. There are times when it seems like everything is against you and far more powerful than you could ever imagine. But with a little work, you can project the confidence that propels you forward and motivates you to put your all into every endeavour.

Finding Your Pride's Origins

1. Prioritise experiences above appearances.
Looks shouldn't be the only factor in determining one's self-worth. Many factors can greatly influence our physical appearance, which is always changing, and various people

have different ideas about what makes someone attractive.

Take pride in something more enduring, such as lessons learned and unchangeable achievements.

2. Embrace the fact that you are human.

Make decisions with pride about your life. Everyone, regardless of age, should follow this guideline in general. When you observe someone who seems successful in everything you want to do, act on it.

Choose a task that will be worthwhile or significant from the available options. Above all, this will raise your sense of self-worth.

❖ Sign up for music courses.

Choose an instrument you've always wanted to play, then start learning how to play it.

You'll feel immensely proud of yourself and accomplished after completing this. Music classes are frequently offered through the neighbourhood centre, universities, high schools, and private instruction, albeit they need time and effort.

❖ Journey.

It is possible to travel for an affordable price. Using youth hostels, taking the train, carpooling, or simply watching for cheap airline tickets can all help you save money. Many amazing things are free to see or take advantage of.

You'll get more self-worth and self-esteem from travelling and have lots of interesting tales to share.

Take up a new sport or artistic endeavour.

Whether you engage in one primarily depends on how busy your mind and body are.

But learning both requires a great deal of effort and time. Even with classes, hands-on learning—especially in groups—is still the most effective learning method.

Playing sports or engaging in artistic endeavours with others is significantly more exhilarating. Engaging in these activities may facilitate easier socialisation and meeting new individuals.

❖ Expand your knowledge anytime you get the chance.

Raise your GPA, consider enrolling in honours courses, and give extracurricular activities your all.

They will benefit you in the long run and make you feel wonderful. If you put up the work in school and attend college, you will have more options to earn money and select careers that are significantly more fulfilling.

3. Take on greater responsibility.

One of the best ways to boost one's sense of value, assurance, and self-esteem is to be responsible. You may prove to yourself that you are capable and positively influence the world by accepting significant responsibilities.

Obtain employment. A job will offer you something more to be proud of and give you money to save for college or spend on items you want.

Look for a job where you can help people, like a health care attendant or a grocery store bagger. You'll feel better about what you're doing as a result.

Offer assistance. Your self-esteem will rise when you volunteer. In the process, you'll frequently improve your skills while helping others.

You may establish a volunteer organisation focused on a cause that matters to you, help at a nearby soup kitchen, construct homes for the impoverished, etc. These kinds of experiences could greatly enhance college applications.

Give directions or instructions to others. You'll feel better about yourself if you help kids and younger children by sharing your life lessons.

Section Six

Reaching your financial objectives

How to maintain motivation

Maintaining your motivation to reach your financial objectives might be difficult, particularly when you encounter obstacles or unforeseen costs. The following advice will help you keep on course:

● Make sensible objectives. When establishing your financial objectives, be honest about how much you can save and how long it will take you to get there. Setting unattainable ambitions will only lead to disappointment and failure.

● Divide your objectives into manageable chunks. Once your financial objectives are established, divide them into more manageable chunks. They will appear more attainable and less intimidating as a result.

Establish a schedule. Make a schedule for when you want to complete each goal after dividing them into smaller segments.

● Monitor your advancement. Maintaining a progress log is an excellent method of motivation. A journal, spreadsheet, or budgeting tool can be used to keep track of your progress. Observing your development over time will keep you inspired and on course.

● Honour your accomplishments. Make sure to celebrate your accomplishments when you meet your financial goals. This will support your motivation to continue pursuing your other objectives.

Advice on getting over financial difficulties

Because of the unpredictability of life, financial difficulties might arise at any time. The following advice can help you get past financial obstacles:

Make a budget. Make a budget if you don't already have one. Earnings and out-of-pocket spending to ensure that you are not exceeding your income.

Reduce your spending. After establishing a budget, carefully review your spending to identify areas where you can save. Perhaps you could cut back on eating out, eliminate any subscriptions you're not using, or compare insurance quotes.

● Look for ways to earn more cash. Should you be experiencing financial difficulties, you might need to look for additional sources of income. You might establish a side business, sell unwanted items, or work part-time.

Speak with your lenders. Speak with your creditors if you struggle to meet your debt payments. They could collaborate with you to create an affordable payment schedule.

Overcoming financial challenges might be challenging but possible with much effort and commitment. Using the above advice, you can overcome your financial challenges and reach your goals.

Here are some more pointers for conquering financial obstacles:

● Ask for help when you need it. If you are having financial troubles, there are a lot of people and organisations who can assist you.

● Keep trying. Overcoming financial issues requires patience and effort. Try not to give up on your financial goals if you encounter obstacles. All you have to do is.

Publicly Funded Pensions

Certain governments—particularly those in Western nations—offer state pensions to help the elderly and those with disabilities finance their retirement. Every such nation has regulations governing who is eligible and to what extent. Social Security, a type of pension the US government offers, is an excellent example. Let's examine the salient features of the government-funded pension schemes in the United States and Spain to understand how they operate.

The State Pension in Spain

The state pension, corporate and employee pensions, and private pensions comprise Spain's pension system. People with disabilities, retired employees, and their surviving spouses are supported financially by the state pension. While practically everyone with a regular salary can apply for a private pension, some firms offer company and employee pensions. We'll be concentrating on state pensions.

Since 2013, Spain's retirement age has progressively increased, and by 2027, it will stand at 67 years old. You can apply for a state pension at 65 years of age and ten months. Over 8.5 million legitimate Spanish nationals contribute to the nation's public pension scheme (MSResidency, n.d.). A qualifying retiree's monthly income ranges from 643 euros ($712) to 2,617 euros ($2,897). The precise amount is determined by variables like the years they have made contributions and their total contributions at retirement.

The good news is that you can continue to get your state pension even if you retire early. However, you must have made contributions for at least 30 years to be eligible for state pension income. Regretfully, to retire early, you must be at least 61 years old (VidaCaixa, n.d.). You will be assessed a certain penalty for making an early claim, even if you retire early.

You can participate in and benefit from Spain's state pension system if you work for yourself.

Social Security in the United States

Old Age, Survivors, and Disability Insurance (AOSDI) programme, also known as Social Security, is a well-known pension system available to retirees in the United States. During the Great Depression, the federal government established this programme to fund elderly workers, their dependents, and impaired individuals. The primary distinctions between this system and Spain's are the amounts and eligibility requirements. About 67 million Americans were expected to receive social security benefits in 2023.

Wherever you work in the United States, Social Security is partly funded by withholding money from your salary. Americans who work for themselves make social security contributions when they file their federal tax returns up to a predetermined amount, often subject to annual revisions. To be eligible for social security benefits in 2023, your annual income must be at least $160,200. Once more, this number could vary annually.

Your income and contributions made throughout your 35 years of greatest earning. It is not feasible to willingly retire young and obtain social security benefits because. The maximum monthly amount you can get if you retire at age 62 is $2,572. This number rises as you get closer to the 70-year limit age (Smith & Ramirez, 2023).

As you can see, the requirement to work for at least thirty years is a major drawback for those who wish to retire early under both the Spanish state pension system and the American social security system. This implies that to be eligible to claim at the minimum age required, you must work for at least that many years. You must work for five to seven years after you retire at age 55 to be eligible for your government's pension programme.

Alternative Plans for Retirement

In addition to pension plans offered by the government, there are private and occupational retirement programmes. First, let's examine occupational pension schemes.

Employers provide defined-benefit (DB) and defined-contribution (DC) retirement plans to their workforce. These initiatives are available in different forms in several nations, such as the United States and Spain.

The most often used schemes in the US are DC schemes. Both the company and the employee must make retirement contributions under these programmes. The most popular of these plans is the 401(k), which enables businesses and employees to contribute pre-tax money from their salary. Employees may postpone taking withdrawals until they reach a specific age, or they may take a lump payment, monthly instalments, or annuities. Taxes are only applied to your retirement funds at this point.

Certain sorts of employment can choose from additional 401(k) plan alternatives. For example, there are 403(b) plans for employees of public schools, universities, and non-profit organisations, and the 457 plan for government employees. There are specific contribution and withdrawal guidelines for each of these programmes. You must comprehend these guidelines to optimise your withdrawals and reduce penalties.

One of the main advantages of defined contribution plans is the ability to contribute with pre-tax income, which maximises the amount of money you put in your pocket. This programme also benefits from having your employer match your payments to a predetermined proportion of your salary. As a result, your retirement funds rise, which may enable you to meet your objective sooner.

You are responsible for choosing investments if you want your defined contribution plan to perform exceptionally well. This could be detrimental if you're not experienced with investing in the stock market. Furthermore, there are restrictions on the kinds of investments you can make.

With DC schemes, you have some control over how your retirement portfolio performs; with DB plans, you don't. In addition to making retirement contributions, the employer makes investment selections on your behalf. The good news is that you will be paid a specific amount each month when you retire. It's critical to comprehend your DB scheme's early retirement policies.

People can also participate in private retirement plans, using their after-tax income to make payments. Because of this, you don't pay taxes on your retirement withdrawals; otherwise, you would pay taxes twice.

The individual retirement account (IRA) is the most widely used private retirement plan in the United States. Regular and Roth. The tax code permits you to write off the amount you contribute to a traditional IRA, but it prevents you from doing the same for contributions made to a Roth IRA. The good news is that no taxes are associated with withdrawals from a Roth IRA.

IRAs are excellent for independent contractors. Even if employed, you can start a private retirement plan to complement your employer-sponsored plan. The largest drawback is that your annual contribution amount is restricted.

-Accredited Purchasers

Preapproved buyers are the best leads you can have when selling your house. These people have already had their bank loan applications accepted before they ever buy a house. You can still sell to purchasers who aren't preapproved, but doing so carries much additional financial risk for everyone involved.

An experienced real estate agent locates suitable, preapproved purchasers for their customers to guarantee that every lead on the house is good.

Real estate agents can access information that indicates whether a lead has been preapproved for a house loan. A buyer's credit report will also be requested.

6) Selecting the Optimal Terms of Sale

Your prosperity is their prosperity when working with realtors. You can be sure that a seasoned real estate agent will use their skill in haggling to get the greatest terms and conditions for your transaction.

Realtors want to profit from the sale, but their main objective is to ensure you are happy with the result. It's crucial to remember that you always have the last word in any situation.

You can find out how a realtor was handled by past clients by reading the evaluations that they routinely leave on some platforms about their encounters with the agent. Since positive evaluations will help them develop, most agents will prioritise their clients above anything else.

7) The Agents' Dos and Don'ts

According to studies, prospective homeowners start looking for a property online at least 12 to 18 months in advance. At this point, they only want information gathering; they don't want an aggressive salesperson contacting them constantly.

You should be conscious of your anxiety regarding your agent. Probably the most significant buying choice you will ever make is this one. Instead of just trying to persuade you to buy, real estate brokers should be able to predict buyer hesitation. You want your agent to patiently and step-by-step assist you.

8) Don't Put Your Clients Under Pressure: Buyers want their real estate brokers to be laid back and not overburden them with details. For example, when customers call, they expect concise, lucid responses. Some agents immediately contact clients, and they continue to call and send them unsolicited emails.

Purchasers of real estate anticipate ethical and professional behaviour from real estate brokers. A competent realtor doesn't bother buyers with follow-up calls or pressure to make impulsive purchases.

9) Do They Post Enough Details and Images of Their Inventory Homes? Before posting your property, you should plan on having many images and videos of it. These should be comprehensive and expert. Interested purchasers will see this first, so it should create a positive impression. The square footage of your house should have the following:

Videos to showcase your house

- Expertly taken pictures of the neighbourhood, leisure activities, and other aspects of the subject's lifestyle
- Comprehensive details regarding the local schools and infrastructure

10) Speak with a Sales Representative

The three primary things you should anticipate from a real estate agent are as follows, which summarise the previously mentioned article:

- Excellent bargaining abilities: Homeowners want to seek representatives with prior expertise. They ought to be able to tell right away how skilled they are at negotiating.
- Communication: Every homeowner anticipates receiving updates from their real estate agent regarding the sale status. They anticipate that agents will notify and update them daily or weekly.

Exchange of ideas.

- Honesty: All clients want their real estate agent to be upfront and honest with them throughout. They object to real estate brokers making false claims to close more deals. They anticipate honesty and openness from agents. This covers their operations, client relations, pricing strategy, appraisal of properties, and other aspects.

Section Six

Setting aside money for important life goals

A big component of financial planning for couples is setting aside money for important life objectives. This chapter will discuss the significance of setting aside money for particular life events, including a down payment on a house, college savings for your kids, and joint retirement planning.

Putting Money Down for a House

For many couples, achieving their goal of homeownership is an important turning point. When saving for a home, a shared vision of your ideal living environment, meticulous planning, and financial discipline are necessary. In this article, we'll discuss the value of saving for a down payment and how to accomplish this shared objective.

The Desire to Own a Home

Similar Goals

A home is a sign of Security, stability, and a location to make enduring memories, so owning one is frequently more than just a financial aim. Your goal of becoming homeowners together provides the framework for the future you two will create.

Deciding on a Reasonable Home Budget

Evaluation of Affordability

Before starting the home-buying process, evaluating your joint financial status is critical. Consider your combined income, current spending, debt payments, and financial objectives. With this evaluation's aid, you can create a reasonable household budget that fits within your means.

The Rule 28/36

amount of debt payments should not be beyond 36%. Following this guideline will assist you in avoiding going overboard.

Establishing a House Fund

The Value of a Household Budget

To become a homeowner, create a savings account only for this purpose. This account will cover relocation expenditures, closing fees, and inspection costs and act as your down payment.

Setting a Goal for the Down Payment

Decide on the desired down payment % after talking it over with others. Typical down payment amounts are between 3% and 20% of the price of the house. The amount of your mortgage and interest payments will decrease with a larger down payment.

Consistent Donations

The secret to increasing your housing fund is consistency. Commit to consistently making contributions, whether it's a monthly donation or something that works better for your budget. By automating these contributions, you can ensure you meet your down payment target on time.

Examining Your Mortgage Options

Knowing About Mortgages

As a pair, familiarise oneself with various mortgage choices. These could include VA, FHA, fixed-rate mortgages, and adjustable-rate mortgages (ARMs). Every option has different terms, interest rates, and requirements for qualifying.

Preapproval of a mortgage

Before looking for a home, think about getting preapproved for a mortgage. Having a mortgage preapproval gives you a set budget, which streamlines your house search and establishes.

Getting Ready for the Costs of Homeownership

Be ready to pay for continuing expenses associated with homeownership, such as utilities, maintenance, and mortgage. You should account for these costs in your entire financial plan and budget.

As a couple, saving for a house is a fulfilling endeavour that shows your dedication to creating a future together. It's about making a place to start your life together, not just buying a piece of land.

Organising for the Education of Children

Giving your kids a top-notch education can be one of your biggest goals as a couple. Careful financial planning is necessary for your children's education to ensure you can support their aspirations and goals. In this part, we'll discuss this objective's significance and how to properly plan for your kids' education.

Taking Care of Aspirations

Your children's education is an investment in their future. It gives them possibilities for both professional and personal growth, as well as information and skills. Your willingness to pay for their education shows how much you care about their achievement and welfare.

Commencing Early

You have more time for your assets to develop the earlier you start thinking about your kids' future education. Compounding is an advantage of starting early that can help you save a lot more money over time.

Advantageous Tax Savings

Examine 529 plans and other education savings accounts, which provide tax benefits for eligible college costs. These programs are a great way to guarantee that your savings grow tax-free while still putting money aside for your kids' education.

Contribution Techniques

After talking it over, decide how much you will consistently give to these accounts. Create a contribution schedule that fits your financial situation and learning objectives. Making consistent contributions is essential to achieving your financial goal.

Selecting the Appropriate Scheme

While choosing an education savings plan, weigh your possibilities. Plans might vary in terms of features and investment options. Examine the terms and benefits of each plan to determine which best meets your family's needs.

Getting Ready for Increasing Education Costs

Counting on Inflation in Tuition

Recognize that inflation causes educational expenditures to increase over time. When forecasting the future costs of your children's education, account for inflation in tuition. This proactive strategy guarantees that you have enough money for future raises.

A Sneak Peek at the S Corporation Concept

After navigating the flexibility of LLCs, let's discuss another type of corporate entity: the S Corporation. "Why is it called a 'S' Corporation?" and "How does it differ from an LLC or a traditional C Corporation?" are probably questions on your mind. You're in the proper place if you're wondering about these things. So, let's work together to clarify the world of S Corporations.

S corporations are similar to chameleons in the corporate ecology. It may take advantage of the greatest features of both corporate and partnership forms by adapting to them. Doesn't it sound intriguing?

The Internal Revenue Code's specific Subchapter S is denoted by the letter "S" in S Corporation. Under this Subchapter, corporations may be taxed as pass-through entities if they satisfy certain requirements. You did hear correctly. Similar to an LLC, a S Corporation is not subject to the double taxation situation that C Corporations are.

Now let's examine some important traits of S Corporations:

Restricted Liability

Above all, like a C Corporation or an LLC, a S Corporation protects its shareholders from personal liability. Hence, your assets will not be available if business takes a dip.

Pass-Through Levy

An S Corporation does not have a corporate income tax rate; instead, profits (or losses) go straight to the shareholders' income, unlike.

Ownership Limitations

Although a S Corporation has many alluring advantages, there are some limitations to be aware of. An S Corporation may have up to 100 investors, but each one must. Various business categories, such as insurance and banking firms, are also excluded from the S Corporation categorization.

Hold on tight if this seems like a whirlwind of information! We will explore the fascinating realm of S Corporations in more detail now. We'll discuss all of them: the drawbacks, the advantages, the ins and outs. After learning each little fact, You'll be better positioned to determine whether an S Corporation is the best option for your company.

But remember that this is only the beginning—a preview. A comparison of S Corporations with other business structures and the complete picture are just around the corner. Remember that every company entity has possible disadvantages in addition to its strengths as we move forward. You must choose the one that best fits your business vision and objectives. All set to resume the journey? Let's explore S Corporations in more detail.

Selecting a S Corporation 2.

Greetings from the intersection. After making it this far, you're prepared to start a crucial phase of your entrepreneurial journey: selecting the best type of company structure. In this chapter, we'll concentrate on one specific option: the mysterious S Corporation.

Recall the fascinating corporate world chameleon we covered in the last chapter. It's time to take a closer look at its vivid colours now. We'll go over the special advantages that set an S Corporation apart from the competition and the drawbacks that can cause you to second guess yourself. Additionally, we will engage in friendly competition between the S Corporation and other commercial entities to see where it excels and where it might fall somewhat short.

Selecting a business structure is not a process that works for every company. For some entrepreneurs, a notable benefit could be a deal-breaker for others. Comprehending your unique business requirements and matching them with the appropriate business entity is essential.

We will don our detective hats and examine the S Corporation from every perspective in this chapter. Whether the advantages of pass-through taxation appeal to you or the ownership limits worry you, we'll answer all of your questions and concerns.

Our goal is to arm. After all, the business operations, taxes, and even your liabilities may be affected by the structure you choose for your company. As a result, it's crucial to give each factor significant thought.

Remember to prioritize your distinct business vision and objectives as we dive deeper into the details of the S Corporation. Ultimately, the company entity that best suits your needs and your business is the one that should be chosen.

Shall we carry on with this investigation now? Next, we'll examine the special advantages of selecting a S Corporation. Prepare to discover the benefits that could make the S Corporation the ideal choice for your aspirations of becoming an entrepreneur.

The Reasons for Selecting a S Corporation The Particular Advantages

Standing at the precipice of choosing the best business structure, the S Corporation offers distinct benefits. It's time to investigate the alluring advantages that could spur your spirit of entrepreneurship and direct you in this direction. Now, let's explore the world of S Corporations and see why it could be the ideal choice for your goals.

Pass-Through Levy

Consider the appeal of a business form that. Exactly what a S Corporation provides is that. Because a S Corporation's profits and losses are carried through to your personal income tax return, it is less likely than a C Corporation to be liable to double taxation. Your tax returns may become simpler, and you may save money on taxes.

Restricted Liability Defense

The restricted liability protection that a S Corporation provides to its stockholders is one of its biggest advantages. This implies that corporate debts and legal liabilities do not threaten your personal assets. Thus, your wealth is protected if an unanticipated event results in financial troubles or legal disputes for your firm.

Reputation and Status

A S Corporation lends legitimacy and professionalism to your firm, which might improve its standing. Potential customers, partners, and investors may feel more confident in your company as a result, seeing it as a well-organized entity with a defined path for expansion and success.

Benefits for Workers

As a S Corporation, you can offer alluring perks to yourself and your staff. This covers retirement programs, health insurance, and other benefits for employees. In addition to offering possible tax savings, these benefits can assist you in luring and keeping excellent staff.

Transferability and Everlasting Being

Compared to other corporate structures, an S Corporation provides easier transferability, making selling or transferring ownership interests easier. In addition, an S Corporation can continue with its business as usual, protecting its legacy.

Though these advantages are alluring, it's vital to remember that they have restrictions and must be considered. For example, there are requirements for becoming a S Corporation, such as being a resident or citizen of the United States and having a maximum number of shareholders. In addition, you have to keep correct records, follow certain procedures, and schedule frequent shareholder meetings.

It is important to consider your unique business objectives, goals, and vision about the special advantages of an S Corporation as you proceed through the decision-making process. Even though an S Corporation might be a good option for many business owners, having expert counsel and considering the long-term effects on your company is important.

We will examine the possible drawbacks of S Corporations and contrast them with alternative business structures in the following sections. Gaining this thorough understanding will enable you to make well-informed decisions supporting your aspirations to become an entrepreneur. Now that we're prepared to explore every facet of the S Corporation experience let's get started.

Creating Alternative Sources of Income

Creating other sources of income might be a great strategy to boost your earning potential and escape the constraints of exchanging time for money. You can produce passive income with little effort and create a more diverse portfolio by generating extra sources of income. The ideal strategy for creating alternative income streams will rely on your resources, hobbies, and skills. There are various ways to do this. Here are some detailed guidelines for creating additional sources of income:

Determine your interests and strengths: Finding your strengths and interests is the first step towards developing profitable side projects. Spend some time reflecting on your strengths and areas of enjoyment. Perhaps you possess a skill set that you could market as a freelancing service or a pastime that you could develop into a business. Think about your abilities, skills, and knowledge. What special benefit can you provide to others?

Which issues are you able to resolve for others? This can assist you in locating possible revenue-generating opportunities. It's crucial to consider your interests as well. What is your favourite activity? Regarding what you have a strong passion for, Investing the time and energy necessary to create a profitable side source of income might be made easier by pursuing a passion.

Look into possible sources of income: After determining your interests and skills, look into possible side sources of money that fit with them. You can begin your investigation into possible sources of income by looking into the market demand for your interests and skill set. Take note of employment trends and pinpoint any opportunities to apply your abilities. Conduct market research to find potential clients, competitors, and price strategies. One of the best ways to find possible sources of money is through networking. Join online communities or go to industry events to meet people who share your interests and abilities; they might know of opportunities or offer insights you would not have thought of.

Determine the most viable and not worth pursuing by evaluating the prospective income and time commitment. Think about the possible revenue streams' sustainability and scalability. Will the income stream eventually produce a consistent flow of income? Is it possible to boost profitability by automating or scaling it up? When assessing possible revenue streams, these are crucial factors to consider. It's crucial to weigh each alternative income stream's potential revenue and time commitment while weighing your options. Find out how much people usually make in the chosen income stream to assess the potential income. Examine the typical prices and charges made by rivals in your sector and the level of demand for the good or service you want to provide. Consider how much time you can commit to your alternative revenue stream when assessing the time commitment. In light of your current job schedule and personal obligations, be cautious not to take on more than you can manage. You can decide which alternative revenue streams are most feasible by weighing the prospective income and time commitment. By doing this, you'll be able to concentrate your efforts on the most promising possibilities and cut down on time spent on ones that are unlikely to result in sizable cash gains.

Make a strategy: Plan how to grow your alternative revenue streams after determining feasible ones. This could entail establishing a website, developing a marketing strategy, and deciding on precise revenue targets.

Start modest:

Gradually gain velocity by starting small.

Avoid attempting to create too many different sources of income at once.

Rather, concentrate on creating one or two sources of income and increase it steadily over time.

Remain arranged: For every additional source of money, keep a record of your earnings and outlays. This will assist you in determining which sources of income are the most lucrative and which ones you should stop pursuing.

Be persistent and patient: Creating alternate sources of income requires work and patience. If you don't notice results immediately, keep trying and being patient. Continue to strive toward your goals with unwavering focus. Beyond regular 9 to 5 occupations, there are many money-earning options. Gives you the freedom and flexibility you want, which is crucial. You can eventually build up several revenue streams and improve your financial independence and security by seeking alternate sources of income.

Investing, freelancing, starting your own business, and passive income streams are all respectable alternatives to working a 9 to 5 job. Here are a few more specifics regarding each choice:

Investing: Investing allows you to make money by making your money work for you. Numerous methods exist, including stocks, bonds, mutual funds, property, and alternative assets like cryptocurrencies or artwork. Investing in assets that will increase in value over time and yield a return on your investment is the idea. While investing has some risks, it may be an excellent method to accumulate money over time. If you're new to investing, it's crucial to.

Freelancing: Working on a project-by-project basis for clients is one way to make money as a freelancer. Freelancers can work in various industries, including writing, design, programming, and marketing. They are usually self-employed. Freelancing offers more freedom and control than regular 9 to 5 jobs. It can also be a wonderful method to establish a portfolio of work that will help you get more clients.

Starting your own business is one method to become an entrepreneur and make money. This can entail producing and selling a good or service online or through a real store. It might also entail purchasing an already-existing company or launching a franchise. The highest level of freedom and flexibility can be found in entrepreneurship, but high risk and labour are involved.

Streams of passive income: These sources of revenue allow one to make money without putting in much effort. This can be accomplished by dividends from investments, royalties from books or music, or rental income from real estate. The goal is to implement a system that, with little to no continuous work on your side, gradually produces income.

Every one of these choices has benefits and drawbacks, and the optimal choice for you will rely on your unique situation and objectives. It's critical to conduct thorough research, consult experts for guidance when necessary, and be ready to put in the effort necessary to succeed.

General Advice

You can apply the product all over your face with gentle circular fingertips.

Moisturizers are a loving gift for your skin. Go for the oil-free moisturizers if your skin is greasy. Use gel-based moisturizers if you have acne, and avoid moisturizers containing perfumes if your skin is sensitive.

Exfoliate your body and face once a week. The finest scrub to use is homemade; don't scrub too vigorously. Choose something soft because your skin is delicate. Gently scrub, then give yourself a water rinse.

Showering with hot water might feel good, but it's best to avoid it. After using hot water, you will get dry skin, scalp, and hair.

Cut it every six weeks. Your hair remains robust and healthy as a result.

Apply mild hair products. Products containing harsh chemicals such as silicones, parabens, sulfates, and so on should be avoided.

Maintain neat, short nails. Long nails are prone to dirt accumulation and can be tempting to bite.

Advice For Women

Hello, ladies. I've been through this stage before, so I know exactly how it feels. You want to appear well, and how you care for your body significantly impacts how you project yourself. Here are some pointers to help you along the way.

Hydrate before taking a shower: Before taking a shower, moisturize with coconut or olive oil. Putting anything between your skin and the shower water prevents your skin from drying out too quickly.

Steer clear of heating tools: Using heated or styling equipment on your hair might be damaging. Avoid wearing styles that require them; use a protective serum if necessary.

Minimize Hair Coloring: Frequently experimenting with hair colour can cause damage to your hair because products that alter its colour can be harsh. If you truly want to, limit it to twice a year.

Guard Your Hair: You need to shield your hair from the sun, salt, and chlorine found in swimming pools. When entering the water, wear a swim cap, and on very sunny days, wear a hat.

Bring on the makeup, please—glossy lips and smokey eyes! While older ladies want to look younger, younger girls want to look older! Here are some cosmetics and beauty advice:

The Key Is Moderation: Overdoing the makeup can undoubtedly result in a makeup disaster. It removes your inherent beauty and is better saved for the stage. When attempting makeup techniques, use moderation. Always keep in mind that simplicity is perfection and that less is more.

Watch for sensitivity: Some sensitive skin may react to certain cosmetics. Thus, use caution and always test product samples before using them.

Take Off Makeup:

Before going to bed, remove all your makeup.

For this, get a mild cleaner, or use a cotton pad and coconut oil.

Recall to be kind!

Allow Skin to Vent: You don't need foundation at this point, believe it or not. Teenagers only need a small amount of lip balm, gloss, and mascara for makeup. Applying rouge and foundation incorrectly might have the opposite effect of what you want and, by clogging your pores, actually cause acne.

Advice For Men

Guys, hey! Skincare and grooming are not just for women. You must have a consistent schedule as well. If you're asking why you should care, you want to maintain your good looks. Of course.

Apply deodorant: Body odour starts to appear as soon as puberty sets in. Thank goodness, someone smart created deodorants. Look for deodorants made entirely of natural chemicals. You can even choose ones with scents to take things a step further.

Locate Your Aroma: But just one smell, okay? And not in buckets! Please limit yourself to one perfume, though you are free to try several until you discover one you enjoy. Use matching cologne and deodorant to avoid conflicting scents. Don't overspend, either. You may believe that multiple sprays are necessary. Believe me. You don't.

Grooming Face Hair: Facial hair grows at varying rates and lengths for men. There's no point trying to 'rock it' like it's full if yours is coming in partially. Simply unwind and give it time to develop. A tidy appearance is not unattractive! If your face is completely hairy, ensure it's neatly shaved and trimmed. Purchase a decent electric shaver, shaving stick, or beard trimmer.

Cleanse and moisturize: Use products designed specifically for males. No, moisturizers and cleansers aren't just for girls!

METHODS FOR A TEEN TO DEVELOP BEHAVIORAL SKILLS.

Select just one ability.

Even though you might want to work on various behavioural skills, choose just one at first so you can focus on it. Select a talent that you believe will help you achieve in life.

For example, you can decide that you want to improve your communication skills so you can effectively provide ideas and proposals in a group setting. If you first concentrate on mastering a single behavioural skill, you might have a better chance of success.

Seek out opportunities to practice.

Once you've selected a behavioural skill, practice it every day, everywhere you go.

If you want to improve your time, for example, prepare a schedule at the beginning of each workday that includes all the tasks and commitments you want to do.

By practising a new skill frequently and developing habits that facilitate learning, you can increase your chances of picking it up. You will find that using a behavioural skill becomes second nature as you get used to it.

Set low expectations.

While acquiring new talent, you might find it helpful to set short-term objectives for yourself as you work toward your long-term objectives. Reaching these small objectives may help you monitor your progress while you focus on picking up a new behavioural skill.

You can start a conversation with a buddy and listen to their concerns or recommendations if you aim to get better at communicating.

Achieving little targets will motivate you to continue developing your behavioural abilities.

Look at other folks.

Many people in your household, school, or area may exhibit the behavioural ability you want to improve.

While you focus on honing your expertise, observe those people to see how they exhibit this proficiency. Then, try to emulate their behaviour in your relationships and day-to-day interactions.

For example, your parents or teacher may be skilled at reaching judgments by seeking advice from others.

By getting to know them better and asking for their opinions, you can try to emulate this behaviour in your own life.

Continue to advance.

It's essential to practice new skills frequently to progress. If you've become more empathetic, you can continue to develop this trait by conversing with friends.

Once you've mastered one behavioural talent, you could keep improving by learning or developing more.

By continuing to improve your behavioural abilities, you may frequently increase your enjoyment eff, effectiveness and productivity.

TEENS' COMMUNICATION SKILLS

Communicating well as a teenager can create wonderful relationships with your parents and peers. Healthy communication is built on truthfulness, listening, respect for others, and being honest about your feelings and desires.

Knowing What Makes for Effective Communication

Speech is not a component of every communication method. Both listening comprehension and respect are essential.

Both sides must communicate healthily. To communicate effectively, you must express your needs and emotions to others while also paying attention to and honouring what others say.

Gaining your way or engaging in manipulation, disdain, or bigotry are NOT components of healthy communication.

Advice for Skillful Communication

Planning and practice are necessary for effective communication. Here are some guidelines to help you get started.

Make use of "I statements."

Be explicit in how you express your thoughts and what you want to be understood; don't say, "You're making me unhappy," but rather, "I feel upset when you do."

Be direct and concise.

Nobody can read your mind, so be honest with others about your needs, wants, and thoughts.

Don't suppress your feelings.

To keep your worries from becoming bigger problems, voice your concerns.

Build a trusting relationship.

Until they offer you a reason not to, you should assume that someone is telling the truth and that they mean well.

Make inquiries.

If you want more information about what someone is saying or their motive, never hesitate to ask questions. Make no assumptions.

Engage in face-to-face communication.

It could be necessary to understand or comprehend an email or SMS message. You can see and hear their body language when you communicate with someone face-to-face or via video chat.

Avoid shouting.

It's okay to become protective or enraged during a discussion. However, it is easier to communicate when you are composed.

Get ready to say sorry.

Everyone makes mistakes from time to time. If you sincerely apologize, moving on after a fight is much simpler.

Teenagers' Need for Effective Communication

You began speaking the moment you were born. Your initial cry served as your first form of speech. On the other hand, communication skills are developed from an early age.

If you are not an excellent communicator, your life will be limited. Thus, developing your communication abilities as a teenager is essential.

With enough practice, communication abilities can be learned and improved like any other talent.

You will advance in various areas by improving your communication abilities, including your career and interpersonal connections.

Developing and maintaining friends is also easier if you have strong communication abilities.

You should communicate with others as an adolescent for the following reasons, among others:

The less trouble you have as an adult, the earlier you learn it.

To say that your upbringing shapes who you become as an adult wouldn't be untrue.

Childhood experiences greatly influence how you respond to situations as an adult.

Teens who acquire strong communication skills at a young age will be more adept at building connections and positive interactions with others.

You learn how to express your annoyance.

A lack of communication skills makes many teenagers susceptible.

Thus, You must communicate well with those in your immediate vicinity, particularly your parents and other caretakers, to open up.

You'll become a better listener by communicating more efficiently.

Excellent communication skills and attentive listening go hand in hand.

1. Recognizing the Hazards

Financially damaging effects of identity theft might include credit harm, bank account depletion, illegal charges, and legal problems. Recognizing the hazards and taking preventative action to reduce them is essential.

2. Safeguarding Private Data a. Safe Passwords: Give each internet account a strong, distinct password. Steer clear of utilizing easily known information like your birthdate, name, or consecutive digits. If you want to create and safely store complicated passwords, consider utilizing a password manager.

b. Safe Internet Use: Exercise caution when disclosing personal information online. Do not enter important information on unprotected websites or click on dubious links. Use safe and encrypted communications when accessing financial accounts or sending personal information.

C. Keep an eye on Your Financial Accounts for any unusual activity. Any unusual activity should be reported right away to your financial institution.

d. Documents to Shred: Before throwing away any documents that include personal information, shred credit card offers, financial statements, and other documents.

3. Monitoring Credit and Fraud Alerts

notify you of any unusual behaviour on your credit report. If someone tries to open credit in your name, add protection. 4. Watch Out for Phishing Attempts

Watch out for phishing attacks, in which con artists pose as reputable companies to steal your data. Unsolicited calls, emails, or messages asking for financial or personal information should raise suspicions. Before disclosing any private information, independently confirm the legitimacy of inquiries.

D. Advice for Preventing Financial Fraud

Awareness of typical financial scams and fraudulent schemes is also essential to protecting wealth. We'll advise you on spotting and avoiding financial fraud in this area.

1. Learn for Yourself

Keep yourself knowledgeable about typical fraud schemes and techniques. To learn how scams work and what warning signals to look out for, do some research on reliable sources and financial institutions. The more information you possess, the more capable you will be to spot and steer clear of con artists.

2. Recognize Unsolicited Offers with Care

Unsolicited offers that promise unique investment possibilities or rapid cash advantages should be considered suspicious. Authentic financial establishments avoid contacting people with unsolicited offers by phone, email, or social media. Before investing any money, thoroughly investigate and independently confirm any investment possibility.

3. Safeguard Personal Data

Refrain from disclosing personal information to unidentified people or groups, including credit card numbers, bank account information, and Social Security numbers. Reputable organizations won't ask for private information over the phone, text, or email unless you want them to. 4. Check Credentials

Check the credentials and qualifications of financial advisors or professionals before interacting with them. Verify whether they hold a license, are registered, or are connected to respectable groups. Make sure they have a solid reputation by looking into their history and reviews.

5. Have Faith in Your Instincts

Trust your gut and proceed with caution if an offer looks too good or you feel pressed for time. Before investing, take the time to carefully investigate and weigh any financial opportunity.

6. Report Supposed Fraud

Report financial scams to the relevant authorities if you encounter them or think you may be a victim of fraud. Contact the appropriate financial regulatory bodies, your state's attorney general's office, and the local police enforcement. By reporting scams, you may safeguard others and improve the offenders' likelihood of being caught.

To sum up, preserving your finances from identity theft, avoiding financial scams, putting estate planning into practice, and knowing what insurance covers are all necessary. Insurance offers crucial financial security against unforeseen circumstances, and estate planning ensures your assets are handled and allocated according to your intentions.

Maintaining vigilance against financial scams helps prevent being a victim of fraudulent schemes while protecting yourself against identity theft helps safeguard your financial assets and personal information. By implementing these tactics into your financial management routines, you may safeguard your financial well-being and preserve your hard-earned assets.

9. Consult an expert.

It might occasionally be quite beneficial to speak with someone whose responsibility is to comprehend you to help you make better judgments.

Whether this person functions as a spiritual director, coach, mentor, counsellor, or some other role, set up regular times to talk with them.

If this individual tells you something about yourself that you don't like or disagree with, keep your cool and hunt for signs in your life that contradict the judgment they gave you.

Give them those cues so they can better comprehend what they've observed and what you're thinking.

Instead of assuming they have you "perfectly figured out," true professionals keep looking into you. And their experience might help you accomplish the same goal.

10. Respond to the questions posed by other people.

You might discover that helping others with their questions gives you a deeper comprehension of your opinions. You can do this quite well on Quora.

You will be disagreed with by many.

No matter what people write, be considerate in your remarks and remember that their feelings are influenced more by their personal experiences and opinions than by you.

Compose your answer as though it were a private letter addressed to the person who had asked it.

Tell the truth, stay focused and transparent (don't stray from the subject), and offer as much support as possible.

11. Permit others to see you when you're most vulnerable.

Don't be afraid to share more of who you are with others, even if doing so means that someone else will have to learn from your mistakes.

You will eventually have to accept that everyone will never like you.

But while some might condemn you for what you say, others might feel less alone in the world due to what you divulge.

12. Compose a mission statement.

First, list your core beliefs (you can get guidance on this site).

Writing down your answer to the question, "What is the single most important goal I want to achieve with my life?" is the next stage.

Alternatively, write your obituary and imagine that a loved one is paying tribute to you as you were before.

Consider what you would like the people you love the most to remember from their time with you.

Consider what keeps you up at night and what drives you to get out of bed in the morning.

Please take a moment to answer those questions honestly as well.

13. Create a vision board, either digital or physical.

Whether you use a poster board, make a slideshow, or post a video on YouTube, creating a vision board may be enjoyable.

Should it be an online vision board application, you may even forward it to those who would benefit from it and inspire them to make one of their own and send it to you. If it's an online vision board application, you can distribute it to individuals who would benefit from it.

Regardless of the medium you are working in, you must try to visualize the life tale you are creating.

For visualization to be effective, you must involve your emotions.

Imagine visualizing leading that life and experiencing every moment of the perfect day.

Additionally, while you go through the experience, observe your feelings and see what comes up for you. Tell the truth and be prepared to modify your plans if needed.

There's no denying that this one is all about you.

Try out several different spiritual instruments.

If there has ever been a nudge in your way toward a certain spiritual practice, be honest with yourself and take the time to learn more about it.

Though you owe it to yourself to learn more, you don't have to dive in headfirst, especially if you were raised with taboos that have kept you from realizing your potential.

Either way, the more you understand the practice, the better you will understand your inclinations.

You will be better informed to decide whether or not to participate if you have more information at your disposal.

So, whatever your thoughts on rune stones, numerology, tarot cards, or anything else related, you should try to follow your intuition as you learn more about it.

mortgage debt

A mortgage is one example of what's seen as "good debt" in this context. Buying a house could ultimately lead to the acquisition of a priceless asset. If that were not the case, this would be a horrible debt! On the other hand, you do not want to purchase a home that is beyond your means and become "house poor."

One of the most crucial lessons in financial literacy that teenagers may learn is the importance of constantly attempting to lower the amount of debt they take on. The alternative is that you will pay a large amount of interest and risk becoming deeply in debt if you don't exercise caution!

9. You ought to begin building credit as soon as possible.

When you think of personal finance for teenagers, it's conceivable that you won't immediately think of having a respectable credit score. On the other hand, if possible, teenagers should begin building credit early.

A better credit score makes getting better financing conditions for large purchases possible. Since most people wish to purchase a car or a piece of real estate with the help of a loan, having a respectable credit score is vital.

You might be able to lower your interest payments by thousands of dollars if your credit score is high.

Furthermore, a high credit score may increase your chances of getting approved for a rental home and help you save money on utilities. Now, the question is, what is the best way to begin building credit? The first thing you should do to ensure identity thieves do not have any open accounts in your name is to check your credit report once a year.

Next, you should consider obtaining a credit card that you can handle sensibly. When you manage your credit well, you avoid exceeding your credit limit and pay all your bills on time and in full each month.

If you're not quite ready to apply for your credit card, think about talking to your. You'll be able to start building credit as a result. Alternatively, you might use a secured credit card to establish your credit history.

10. Use all of your resources to achieve financial success.

There is a shift happening in the world. As a teenager, you must deal with the challenge of making money in a completely new setting.

The good news is that creative entrepreneurs now have many more possibilities to follow their goals thanks to these changes. You should look into the option of launching your own business to ensure your financial security in the future. It is possible to start a business without any financial backing; financial resources are not even strictly necessary.

Yet another creative way to get money is through house hacking. Under this plan, you would pay a monthly deposit to cover the down payment on your first adult home.

You should begin looking for roommates when you purchase the property to divide the mortgage payments. If you apply this method, you can build equity in a home without devoting a significant amount of your income to the mortgage payment.

As you understand financial literacy for teenagers, set a creative goal for yourself: consider how you could incorporate the concepts of responsible money management into your own life.

EDIT YOUR RESUME AND CAREFULLY GET READY FOR JOB APPLICATIONS

Customize Your Resume for the Job: Review the job description and note the essential competencies and abilities the company is looking for.

Make your CV unique by emphasizing accomplishments, experiences, and pertinent abilities that match the position's needs.

Employ a Simple and Professional Format: Make sure your resume is easy to read and browse by keeping it simple and well-organized.

Ensure you have proper headings and sections, a professional typeface, and a consistent layout.

Add a synopsis or goal statement:

A summary or objective statement emphasizing your major skills and career ambitions should come first on your resume.

Adapt this section to the particular position for which you are applying.

Highlight Your Achievements and Skills: Provide a special skills section focusing on pertinent hard and soft abilities.

When summarizing your achievements, use bullet points to highlight the quantifiable outcomes and significance.

Give a Detailed Employment History: Commence with your most recent position and arrange your work history chronologically.

Provide your job titles, business names, and employment dates, and briefly explain your accomplishments and responsibilities.

Emphasize Your Education and Certifications: List your degrees, certificates, relevant experience or courses, and educational background.

Emphasize any accolades, distinctions, or academic successes.

Include Relevant Keywords: To make your CV stand out to applicant tracking systems (ATS), include pertinent keywords and phrases from the job description.

This can increase the likelihood that hiring managers will evaluate your resume in more detail.

Verify the Resumé for Accuracy and Clarity: Look for spelling, grammar, and punctuation mistakes.

Make sure the details convey your qualifications in an accurate and up-to-date manner.

Write a Professional Cover Letter:

Provide a strong introduction.

Explain why you are interested in the job.

Showcase your experiences and relevant talents in your cover letter.

Make each cover letter unique to the position you're applying for.

Assemble the supporting documentation.

Assemble any other supporting materials the company may request, such as a portfolio of your best work or reference letters and transcripts.

Make sure these documents are professionally formatted and orderly.

Observe Application Instructions: Adly adhere carefully to the employer's application guidelines.

Within the allotted time, submit your application documents using the designated means (online application, email, or postal mail).

Seek Input and Ongoing Enhancement:

Consult with mentors, real advisors, or other reliable people for input on your application materials and résumé.

Update and tweak your resume often to reflect your growing experience and skill set.

You may improve your chances of getting hired and an interview by improving your resume and professionally preparing your job applications. A strong application package and CV can showcase your skills, project a polished image, and show that you are a good fit for the role you're applying for.

To summarize, applying for jobs and polishing your resume entails customizing it for the position, using an organized and professional format, adding a summary or objective statement, highlighting accomplishments and skills, giving a thorough employment history, emphasizing education and certifications, adding pertinent keywords, editing your writing for accuracy and clarity, crafting a formal cover letter, obtaining supporting materials, adhering to application guidelines, getting feedback, and always improving. You may improve your chances of being noticed as a strong applicant and landing the desired jobs by devoting time and energy to preparing your job application materials.

Keep aside for emergencies.

Your financial condition may improve if.

Circumstances like the need for significant home repairs.

One of your objectives may be to increase your savings. If so, you might want to think about using this financial advice to aid with unforeseen costs:

Recall that interest rates can change: It can be prudent to compare prices. The additional interest can increase over time if you discover a savings account with a higher rate.

Invest additional funds in your account: Think about transferring money into your bank account when you receive a bonus at work or a tax refund. The additional funds can increase your savings.

Invest in necessities instead of wants.

Before making a purchase, research and determine whether you truly need the item or could live without it. If you truly believe you need it, compare in-store and online prices so you may use the remaining funds for savings.

Configure your savings to happen automatically.

You might be able to increase your savings without giving in to the need to spend extra money by setting up automatic transfers to your savings account with your employer's assistance.

Put money aside for major purchases.

Being able to postpone gratification can greatly improve your financial management skills. By delaying big purchases, you allow yourself more time to consider whether they are necessary and more time to research prices instead of forgoing other necessities or charging the item with a credit card. Suppose you save money instead of using credit. You won't have to cope with the numerous repercussions of missing payments if you save money instead of ignoring duties or invoices.

Put money aside for the future.

Aim to always have at least three to six months' worth of living expenses saved. The minimum amount of money you should have on hand in emergencies is three. Still, many financial advisors even advocate going further and saving for at least nine or twelve months. You only spend this money in dire circumstances, such as when you must pay for medical expenses or lose your work.

What monthly fixed and necessary expenses do you have? Calculate your minimum emergency savings by multiplying this amount by three to six months.

List the things you want to save. Are you thinking about taking a trip to Aruba or retiring next year? The monthly amount you must save will vary significantly depending on your goals. List the things you wish to save for, their associated prices, and the months before they happen. Say you have a new job and need to buy a car in the coming year. You've set your sights on a $5,000 used car, and the work will begin in six months. Accordingly, you must set aside about $834 a month to pay for the car.

Plan your holiday spending five to six months in advance. Even $50 a month will give you a $300 present cushion by December.

You can never start saving for your children's college education early enough. When kids are born, open individual savings accounts and prioritize saving.

Make consistent savings contributions.

Making a monthly contribution to a savings account can assist you in developing sound financial practices. It is also possible to program the system to move funds automatically from your checking account to your savings account. In this manner, you won't need to recall to make the move.

If saving is difficult, take out the cash you can spend now.

Taking out the entire amount you need to spend in cash at the start of the month is one of the best strategies to prevent overspending when money is tight. To ensure you know precisely how much you have, divide it into envelopes, one for each category, such as food, gas, rent, etc. Debit and credit cards should be left at home. It is much simpler to just swipe a credit or debit card without considering how much a product will cost. You are far more likely to halt before purchasing a non-essential item if you must pay the same amount in cash each time.

Putting your money to use

When your savings begin to increase, you can increase the amount you contribute to your pension; this is an excellent method to ensure you can live a more comfortable retirement.

Create an investment strategy that takes your time and goals into account.

Chapter 7: Budgeting

Additionally, it enhances the chapter's appeal.

Financial planning must include saving money; it is never too late to start. Sound-saving habits can help you achieve your financial objectives more quickly. In this chapter, we'll look at some money-saving strategies and how to lay a strong financial foundation.

Establish Savings Objectives

Establishing clear, quantifiable goals is the first step towards saving money. It's critical to be reasonable and consider your financial circumstances while establishing your savings objectives. Determine your goals for saving first, whether it's retirement, a down payment on a house, or an emergency fund.

Next, determine how much you need to save and establish a deadline for finishing the task. Divide your objective into more achievable, smaller milestones, and acknowledge each as you pass it. If you do this, you'll stay motivated and on course to accomplish your final goal.

Establish a Budget

Budgeting is essential if you want to save money. You can monitor where your money is going and find areas where you can save by using a budget. Once you have a month's worth of expenses, divide them into fixed and variable costs.

Variable expenses include groceries, entertainment, and eating out, while fixed expenses include rent or mortgage payments, auto payments, and insurance fees. Seek opportunities to reduce your variable costs and apply those savings to your desired savings amount.

Put Your Savings in Motion

Automating your savings is a very simple approach to saving money. You may ensure you automatically save a certain amount each month without realizing it.

Consider opening a different savings account if you're saving for a certain objective. Doing this allows you to monitor your development and keep that money separate from other needs.

Cut Down on Debt

Debt reduction is essential if you want to save money. Deplete your savings and keep you from achieving your financial objectives. Pay the debt with the highest interest rate first, then proceed down the list.

A reduced interest rate can be a good option for consolidating your debt. By doing this, you may pay off your debt more quickly and save money on interest.

Reduce Your Expenses

Reducing spending is another excellent method of saving money. Look for places to cut costs, including entertainment, eating out, or subscription services. To save money on food and home goods, and discounts.

Make little lifestyle adjustments that will build up over time. A year if you pack your lunch for work rather than eating out every day.

Launch a Side Business

You might earn extra cash by starting a side business to contribute to your savings objectives. There are several ways to earn extra money in your leisure time, such as dog walking, online sales, and freelancing.

When selecting a side gig, take your hobbies and skills into account. Also, be honest about how much time you can devote to it. Over time, even a $100 weekly wage increase can result in sizable savings.

Monitor Your Development

It's important to monitor your progress if you want to save money. Staying motivated and making necessary modifications can be facilitated by often reviewing your savings objectives and spending plan.

Consider utilizing a savings tracker to keep track of your progress toward your savings objectives. An app that automatically tracks your savings or a basic spreadsheet can be used for this.

In summary

By establishing clear objectives and a budget.

www.ingramcontent.com/pod-product-compliance
Lightning Source LLC
Chambersburg PA
CBHW052152110526
44591CB00012B/1947